100 Ways to Motivate Kids

100
Ways to
Motivate Kids

JULIE POLANCO

NASHVILLE

NEW YORK • LONDON • MELBOURNE • VANCOUVER

100 Ways to Motivate Kids

Published in New York, New York, by Morgan James Publishing. Morgan James is a trademark of Morgan James, LLC. www.MorganJamesPublishing.com

The Morgan James Speakers Group can bring authors to your live event. For more information or to book an event visit The Morgan James Speakers Group at www.TheMorganJamesSpeakersGroup.com.

ISBN 978-1-64279-123-5 paperback
ISBN 978-1-64279-124-2 eBook
Library of Congress Control Number: 2018906769

Cartoons by:
Sofia Polanco

Cover Design by:
Rachel Lopez
www.r2cdesign.com

Interior Design by:
Bonnie Bushman
The Whole Caboodle Graphic Design

In an effort to support local communities, raise awareness and funds, Morgan James Publishing donates a percentage of all book sales for the life of each book to Habitat for Humanity Peninsula and Greater Williamsburg.

Get involved today! Visit
www.MorganJamesBuilds.com

For curious kids everywhere. You were made
to run, to explore, to create, to care.
Go out and fulfill your God-given purpose!

Table of Contents

Acknowledgements

I would like to thank my editor, Trinity McFadden, for her help in making this book the best it could be. Margo, Nikkole, David, and Jim—you're the best. Special thanks to my dear family for testing some of these ideas and proving their worth. And most of all, thanks to my Lord Jesus for answering my prayers as I wrote.

How to Use This Book

Welcome, parents!

This book is not like any other "activity" book out there. The ideas contained in this book are designed to help your children—ages 6 and up—draw on their intrinsic motivation to learn. All of them are developmentally appropriate *if implemented for the age indicated.* For ages 8 and up, the ideas are tied to school subjects to help children make the connection between what they learn in school and in real life. If you are a homeschooler, you can easily integrate many of these ideas into your curriculum.

The goal of *100 Ways* is to help your children develop higher order thinking skills and STEM skills and to feed their God-given passions. Please do not use this book as an assignment.

Allow your child to choose options that interest him and assist him in making them happen, as needed. Some of the ideas are more time-intensive than others and some will be more successful with the help of friends.

Most of these activities are technology free and encourage you and your child to participate in your community.

You will see that each idea leaves room for your own creativity and can be adapted to your situation. I generally do not include specific directions on how to make things such as egg paint, slime, or Rube Goldberg machines. There are already plenty of resources out there for these directions, and you can find them on my Pinterest page as well (my username is jpolancobooks).

Go out and have fun!

(*By the way, my kids appear in this book from time to time. Their names have been changed to protect their privacy. They appear as "Tiger," "Hawk," "Butterfly," and "Mouse."*)

Ideas for Children Ages 6 to 7

Most children under the age of 8 don't need motivation to learn. This section includes ideas for children who are 6 and 7 years old. They may not be appropriate for children younger than that because of developmental differences. It is important for little children to play most of the time, so even these suggestions are for enriching play activities. You will notice that there are many ideas for active youngsters. Small children can be harmed by too much sitting, looking at screens, and formal classes. God made a wonderful planet for us to care for and enjoy. Get them outside!

. . . .

Outdoor Ideas

. . . .

Unstructured outdoor time is the best antidote to offer to restless, bored, curious children. The best setting is a wild one, but if you don't live near wild places (even a forest preserve will do), a park is still better than looking at a screen. The complexity of nature, the fresh air and life-giving dirt, the lessons God offers—all these are essential for a happy, peaceful child. Here are a few ideas to help their exploration.

1. Play "magnifying glass" outdoors. You don't even need to have a magnifying glass to do this. You can use a frame of any sort, even the one formed by touching the tips of your index fingers and thumbs together. The idea is to ask them to tell you all that they find within that frame. For example, he might go out and choose a spot near some trees or bushes. Then he waits quietly. Are there insects that appear? Leaves? Maybe a squirrel or bird? Encourage him to see if he can find more. Five things? Ten things? Help him develop patience and the powers of observation.

2. Outdoor scavenger hunt. This doesn't need much explanation. Give your child a list of items to find and see how many she can find. If there are several children who are old enough to play, then they can make a game of it.

3. Visit an animal farm, vegetable farm, or orchard. Some of you may do this already, especially pumpkin patches and apple orchards. Why not schedule a tour of a local organic farm or visit a farmer's market and talk to the farmers? What about a local working ranch? Better yet, grow a small garden, even just one tomato plant, yourself.

4. Nature Art. Gather some pinecones, pine needles, cattails, tall grasses, twigs, palm leaves, or whatever you can find in your area. What can you create with these items? Can you imitate how a bird makes her nest? How about a mouse bed? What about imaginary creatures, like fairy homes?

5. Who's out in winter? You may already explore the landscape in winter, but what about looking for footprints and scat? What other signs of life can you find? Not all animals leave in the winter. Many birds and other creatures are still active. Challenge your young child to look for clues of life, sit and watch for the creatures, and discover more about them when you get home. Don't forget the hot chocolate!

Art and Imagination Ideas

Most kids this age love art of all sorts—visual, performance, and written. Let's move beyond crayons and tempera paints and try some unique projects that get them thinking in new ways about materials around them.

1. Build big with boxes. Grocery stores, moving companies, restaurants, and department stores all receive boxes of goods every day. Let the manager know that you are collecting them and ask if she would set some aside for you. Bring them home and offer ideas for what they could become. Castle? Playhouse? Ship? Let them dream up something.

2. Expand your art supplies. Try painting with egg paint. You can find instructions online at sites such as

Instructables. Basically, it's egg yolk, vinegar, pigment, and water. Try using fruits and dye some old white T-shirts or handkerchiefs. What about old coffee grounds to make those imaginary maps look aged?

3.What would your stuffed animal do? Encourage your child to move beyond the usual play scenarios of tea parties, mommies, attack raids, and bad guys. Throw out some other possible problems such as: What would the dolls do if the stuffed animals wanted to live in their house? Or what if the bad guys took all the animals? Or what if. . .? Come up with some other ideas.

4. Make your own simple card or board game. All games have a clear objective to decide the winner. How is your winner decided? By the most cards, most points, or who reaches the end first? You can use index cards if you make a card game or use a file folder for a board game. Easy card games can be matching or memory. Board games can use cards or spinners to move forward, with "trick" or "prize" spaces. There are lots of ideas for these on my Pinterest page at jpolancobooks.

5. They're pants, now they're skirts, now they're capes. Ever hear of play silks? These are large pieces of naturally dyed silks for use in children's dress up games. Instead of purchasing costumes, you can use old sheets cut down to about three to four large squares. There are two downsides to using cotton or flannel sheets, though. One, they can be heavy, and, two, they are harder to tie at the corners than lightweight silks. Using silk doesn't need to be expensive. Remember, the premise of this book is that all ideas are low or no cost. Look online for wholesale silk chiffon squares at places like Dharma Trading Company or Alibaba. One large square usually costs $5 to $10 (not the toy catalog price of $20 to$30). Sometimes you can even receive large sample squares for free. Get them in white, and dye them different colors yourself, using Kool-Aid packets. Or try looking for large women's fashion scarves at thrift stores. Some of them are large enough to blanket a small child, and that is just the size you need. Your children may be puzzled at first by a box of large pieces of fabric, but soon they will be using them for clothing, forts, beds, and whatever else they can dream up.

. . . .

Storytelling and Language Ideas

. . . .

A lot of children ages 6 to 7 years old don't read well. Some do but may not enjoy writing. These ideas take that into account and encourage them to narrate their ideas and to explore words in new ways.

1. Finish my story. Start telling an oral made-up story and stop at an exciting point. Ask your child, "What happens next?" Let her tell the next part and ask her to leave off at another exciting point. You pick it up from there and see how imaginative and silly you can be together.

2. Invented words. Do you know how many new words are invented each year? Just think: When I was a kid, the words "e-mail," "social media," and "Internet" didn't exist. Kids love silly words. Together, play with words and come up with some silly new names for common items or activities. The poem "Jabberwocky" by Lewis Carroll is a great example of this. See where this leads you.

3. "Tell me with your mouth." When my son Mouse was little, he didn't want me to read stories. He wanted me to make them up myself and to tell them "with my mouth." Oral storytelling is enjoying a bit of a comeback. Perhaps your child would enjoy listening to you—or someone else he loves—tell him a story. Does Grandma live 100 miles away? Maybe she could record herself telling (or retelling) a story and send it along to your child. Give him a pad of paper and crayons, but don't force him to draw. Just allow him to use the paper as he is inspired while he listens. This not only encourages him to learn to listen carefully, it also helps him picture things in his mind, forges family bonds, and inspires him.

4. Quote of the day in an unusual way. For a while, I posted a new Bible verse or famous quote on the wall in the bathroom. I posted it in a strategic place so that my kids (or anyone else using the bathroom) couldn't help but read it while they were in there. I made sure that it was worded using vocabulary they could read. This not only helped them learn Bible verses; it also helped them remember things like, "I can do all things through Christ who gives me strength"

(Philippians 4:13) and, "If God is for us, who can be against us?" (Romans 8:31). Build your child up by reminding him of who he is and who is with him. Nothing can be more motivating than that.

5. Photo captions. Does your child love to take photographs with your phone? Why not create a folder just for her and ask her to write captions for the photos she takes? Offer to help with the typing or, if she wants to type, be on standby for spelling questions. This is a great way to use her interest to motivate her, but keeping it casual, not forced.

Ideas for Exploring People and Places

Children this age often have rudimentary, mythical ideas of how people in other countries live and about what they are like. Thinking about abstract concepts, like living on a planet or places drawn on a globe, is difficult for them. However, these same kids are certain about things that are completely imagined, such as Santa Claus (although he is based on an actual historical figure), the tooth fairy, and leprechauns. We can work with that to help them understand the needs of others.

1. Design an imaginary place. Kids seem to know a lot about unicorns, fairies, and other mythical creatures. Ask your child questions about where they live, what they eat, what they do for fun, what their holidays are, etcetera. Then ask them to come up with a totally new creature. Ask them to come up with answers to those same questions for the new creature.

2. Create a map of a place from a favorite story. Let's say your son's favorite story is "Saint George and the Dragon." Ask him to draw the castle, the countryside, where the dragon lives, where George was found by the fairies, etcetera. You could show him examples of real maps, especially the ones used in zoos and museums, since he is familiar with the exhibits and the buildings. This is especially fun if the map is made from edible items.

3. I live in a yurt, and you live in a pueblo. Tell your child that you found out about an unusual type of house called a yurt. What does she think that is? Look it up together and talk about how the people made the house. Would she like to live in a house like that? What might that be like? Does she know of any houses that are similar? (You can do this same exercise with other types of houses, like pueblos, pile dwellings, stilt houses, or an earth berm house.) Your child will be fascinated by how others live and may be inspired to build a pretend one just to experience it for herself.

4. Some people play with their thumbs. What type of instrument do you play with your thumbs? Can you play an instrument with your feet? Look at the kalimba, cajón, and other ethnic instruments. Can you make some at home? Borrow some recorded world music from the library.

5. Mufaro had a beautiful, rough-faced girl named Cinderella. Other cultures around the world have different ways of telling a familiar fairy tale. Have you ever read *Mufaro's Beautiful Daughters*, *The Rough-Face Girl*, or *Adelita*? These are all Cinderella tales from around the world. Reading an alternative telling of the same fairy tale can often start conversations about cultures your child hasn't encountered. It can sensitize them to the fact that everyone shares the same struggles with friendship, belonging, and love. You could also read *Pretty Salma* and *Lon Po Po,* which are multicultural tellings of the Red Riding Hood story.

Ideas for Exploring Math

hildren this age are just starting to move into understanding math concepts from representational pictures. They do not understand abstract math concepts that do not relate to their immediate lives. I've seen this happen a lot. My daughter Butterfly could do worksheet math but did not see the connection to her daily life. Conversely, she could do suggestion number one below in her head, but not on paper. I ended up ditching the worksheets.

1. How many days is it until. . . Your birthday? Christmas? Our vacation? How many weeks is that? How many cupcakes will we need to make? How many cookies? Use significant events in your child's life to give him an awareness of how math is used.

2. How many are in my hand? I played this game with Tiger and Butterfly when they were little. They loved it! Place a certain number of beans in front of your child. Let's say it's 12. Secretly, you put 5 in your hand (make sure she doesn't know how many are in your hand). Say: "I have some beans in my hand. I'm going to take 7 beans from the pile." (Not from her pile of 12.) "Now, I have the same number of beans that you have. How many did I have to start?" Kids love secrets and solving mysteries. You can play this type of game over and over with different amounts. It helps her learn basic algebra, too.

3. My hands are as wide as I am tall! How many mathematical facts does your child know about his own body? Stretch out your arms and say something like: "See. This is how tall I am." He will probably give you a puzzled look. Then you say: "You don't think so? Let's find out!" Get out your measuring tape and let him measure and compare. This is a starting point for other measurements. How long is your head? How many of those are you tall? How does the length of your arm compare to the length of your leg? This is a fun and interesting way to practice measuring, counting, and comparing.

4. The tall glass and the fat glass are the same size. Children this age think that something short doesn't hold as much as something tall, even if the short item is fat. Intentionally pour a measured cup of juice into a tall glass and the same amount into a shorter, fatter glass. Offer the two glasses to your young children. They will likely complain that one has more. This is your chance to prove that it isn't true. Then move on to other types of containers, such as putting the same amount of macaroni and cheese into a large bowl and into a smaller bowl. It will seem to them that the smaller bowl contains more. Again, prove it isn't so. They will likely find this fascinating, even if they are still a bit suspicious.

5. A person is four rectangles, a square, a triangle, and a circle. You child knows his shapes, but can he find them in unusual places? What shapes can he find in a house plant? His shirt? The car? Make a game of it. Who can find six circles as we take a walk to the park? How many hearts can you find in the garden? Help your child relate shapes to more than the obvious table or plate. Artists use this technique to sketch, and you can use it, too, to build greater awareness of the world.

 # Ideas for Children Ages 8 to 12

Children this age are generally very competent. They are in the developmental stage called "Industry" and want to know how to do almost anything. However, motivation can start to lag right around this time. This can happen because of overscheduling, boring and irrelevant schoolwork, and disregard for the child's passions. The ideas in this section are meant to rekindle the dying embers of your child's passions, build confidence, and challenge her thinking and creativity.

Language Arts

While children this age know how to read, they may struggle with composition skills. They may need some encouragement in their communication skills. These suggestions focus on giving kids reasons to share with others in a meaningful way, not with emoticons, acronyms, and shorthand. We need to take back our most valuable human asset—written language—and it starts with our children. Let's engage our kids in face-to-face time and immerse them in longer reads.

1. Take them to the library (or bookstore) and let them choose whatever books they want. This idea may not seem all that amazing, but consider how often we choose books *for* them. There are many reasons why we may do this, but think about what we are saying to our children when we don't allow them to choose. We are saying that we don't trust them to make good choices, that only *we* know what good books are, and that our interests are more important than theirs. Let them choose, even if they choose gross joke books, graphic novels (although you might want to check the images), or fashion magazines. They won't choose those things every time, and their choices can spark some great conversations.

I did this with my daughter Tiger when she was twelve, and she chose books I didn't like. However, the books sparked conversations about worldview, pop culture and trends, multiple perspectives, and more. It also drew us closer together, because I showed her that I respected her as a person.

2. Create a traveling notebook. Purchase a bound notebook and write some notes about your child and your time together. End your note with an open-ended question for your child to answer and to keep the conversation going. For example: "I really enjoyed our time at the movie today. It was fun to stuff our faces with popcorn and laugh together. What was your favorite part of the movie?" After a month or two, maybe longer, you will have a keepsake of your thoughts and written conversations. What a wonderful way to document your child's life.

3. Put together a family newsletter. Let your child interview you and take pictures. Encourage her to imagine what your pets might say. Let her make it as silly and funny as she likes. Include jokes and cartoons that she creates. Perhaps all your children can work together and then send it to extended family members, such as grandma and grandpa.

4. Do you say "it's" or "its"? Get a cereal box or other kid favorite (maybe the box from a recent toy purchase) and ask your child to rewrite the advertising copy on the outside of the box or to rewrite the assembly instructions. They get to intentionally forget punctuation, use the wrong homonym, and spell incorrectly. The more mistakes they make, the better. This gets lots of laughs, but it also helps them spot the frequent public errors in spelling and punctuation that are rampant these days. They will gain a new appreciation for why these aspects of language are important.

5. Rewrite the ending. Ever hear of fractured fairy tales? This is a bit like that. What if Goldilocks didn't run away from the three bears? What if Cinderella didn't have the other glass slipper? Explore different endings for popular, and not-so-popular, stories. Did a different character become the hero or heroine, or did the main character find a different route to obtaining their goal or desire?

6. It didn't happen that way; it happened this way. This is similar to number five, but this time retell the story from a different perspective, such as telling the story of the three little pigs from the wolf's perspective (there is a hilarious version of this available called *The True Story of the Three Little Pigs* by Jon Scieszka). *Maleficent* is another example. How does the story change when you do this?

7. Oh, balderdash and nincompoop. Find funny sounding words in your dictionary that aren't really used anymore—the funnier, the better. Make a list of them. Discover their true meanings together and then choose one to use often throughout the day. This is different than inventing new words, like in *Frindle* by Andrew Clements. This is about using real words that no one uses anymore, making life interesting, and helping children gain an appreciation for the power of having the precise word for what you are trying to say. Too often, I have heard people say things like, "You remember that place, that place with the big thing in front of it?"

8. Did I get any mail today? Create a "mailbox" for each member of the family. Put "mail" for them in their box, things like thank you notes for doing a great job on something or helping out, short stories you think they might like, or just a letter to them about your day together. You could even mail them a letter for real. Kids love getting mail, and they will be inspired to write back to you. These notes can be the start of a scrapbook. My daughter Butterfly really latched on to this idea and put a lot of effort into decorating her box. She also created boxes for each of her three siblings and insisted that everyone put little notes in her box. It has been fun giving each other encouragement and sharing laughs.

9. Library scavenger hunt. What better way is there to help your children learn how to find treasure? First, determine which books you want them to discover. Start with five and find them yourself first so that you can create appropriate clues. Then create riddles that lead them to your titles. This will help them learn to navigate your library, be resourceful, and find new favorites. For more fun, let them make a scavenger hunt for you!

Are you enjoying these ideas? Tell others! Leave a review on your favorite bookstore's website.

• • • • • •

Math

• • • • • •

Did you turn to this section first? Everyone seems to have trouble motivating their kids to do math. Who wants to sit in a chair and do rows and rows of math problems? No one. There is the argument that kids need practice in order to perfect their computation abilities. However, if they don't understand how it's used in real life, their perfect computation won't matter. Math is a tool, not a subject. Just like any other tool, it gets sharpened by using it in real situations. Here are some ideas to motivate your child to use the skills he has learned in his own ways.

1. Let your child plan a party for a few friends. What kid doesn't like having a fun time with friends? The key here is that you set the budget but tell her to plan it. She will need to decide on plates, cups, napkins, treats, and everything else. Do not help her, except to say, "Did you remember that you need _____?". Insist that she figures it all out herself. Not only will this build self-confidence, but she also will need to use a lot of math to figure it all out and the consequences will be real. If there is not enough of something, she will learn troubleshooting skills as well.

2. What can you buy with $10? Give your child $10 and a short list of items to buy at the grocery store. Let him do the shopping and do not help him, except maybe to remind him about sales tax. Let him do all the math. Try it with $20 the next time and see how he does. Variations of this idea might be going to a thrift store instead of the grocery store, or buying Christmas presents with a limited amount of money. Not only do kids get to practice their math, they also learn something about budgeting.

3. How many gerbils will there be in one year? Do you have gerbils, hamsters, or rats? What about a cat or a dog? How many babies can they have in one litter? How long does it take for those babies to mature and have litters of their own? How many litters can a gerbil have in one year? Many children are interested in this question, and, even if the math isn't quite accurate, they will get a sense of exponents through this very tangible activity. Not only that, they will begin to grasp the enormity of the rodent problem. This can get pretty complicated, so it may be helpful to create a diagram.

4. We're going on a day trip. Pretend that you are going somewhere that is less than three hours away. I live near Chicago, so I might pretend I am going to Rockford, Illinois, for the day. I would ask the kids how far away that is. For the first 50 miles of the trip, I can drive 60 mph, and, for the rest of the trip, I can drive 70 mph. How long will it take to get there? If gas costs $2.56 per gallon and the car gets 19 miles per gallon, how many gallons of gas will I use? If I started with half a tank, will I need to refill it before I drive home? Substitute your own cities and numbers. To make it especially fun, actually go there!

5. Oh, no, the 1/4 cup measure is gone! Want to make fractions relevant? Allow your child to make cupcakes from scratch with one or more measuring cups missing. The best ones to hide are the ones used most frequently: 1 cup, 1/2 cup, or 1/4 cup. You could also try hiding the teaspoon or 1/2 teaspoon measure instead. This is a fun and delicious way to see how well your child understands the relationships between the most common fractions.

6. Which bucket should I buy? Classic Lego bricks measure 15.8mm x 31.8mm x 9.6 mm. If I wanted to make a tower that reached to my ceiling, and it was 30mm square, would the 790-piece bucket be enough? What if I wanted to make a house for our cat that was 30mm x 90mm x 60mm? Should I buy the 790-piece bucket, or will I need the 1,200-piece bucket?

7. What does a .33 batting average mean? Explore how sports statistics are calculated. For example, in basketball, how are effective field goal percentages calculated? In baseball, how are batting averages calculated? How are completion percentages figured in football? What about other sports? Why are these stats important? This also can lead to interesting discussions about human skill, such as why a batter can miss two out of three times and still be considered good.

Social Sciences

Children this age start to become interested in the world and understand that things were happening before they existed. They can comprehend that we live on a planet with many different cultures that are different from their own. Many children are eager to learn about others, but it still needs to be in concrete, sensory ways. This is a great age for children to engage with museums, reenactments, and crafts. Here are a few ideas to supplement your adventures.

1. Bring home a "mystery fruit" from the grocery store. Leave it on the table and see if anyone asks what it is. When their curiosity is piqued, then it's time to ask more questions! What is it? Where does it grow? How does it grow? How do people prepare it? The best part is actually eating it, of course, and discovering a new favorite! Make a regular habit of doing this and discovering where food comes from and how people of those countries eat.

2. Grandma's special treasures box. Grandma and grandpa may have lived through some of the most tumultuous times in our nation's history. Kids sometimes get bored just listening to people talk, but they will respond well to matching live objects to a story. Ask your parents if they have some treasures from their youth, such as military medals, pictures, books, clothes, and other paraphernalia that they wouldn't mind using as props to talk about some of those things. Kids want to know what it was like in a tangible way, and not just be told names and dates.

3. Visit ethnic neighborhoods. Even if you don't live in a city, I bet you live near one. Most cities have ethnic neighborhoods. Explore. Go inside the shops and ask questions about their wares. Why do Chinese stores have dragons and Buddha statues? Why do people from parts of Ethiopia eat with their hands from a common bowl? Variations of this are visiting ethnic restaurants or cooking ethnic food at home.

4. 3D map of the United States (or wherever you live). This will require a large poster board, clay or similar material, and some other odds and ends. Print an enlarged map of your country and paste it to the poster board. You may need a physical map to help you, but the idea is to use the clay and other materials to create a 3-D map of your country. Include mountains, lakes, forests, swamps, deserts, and more. Try to make it as accurate to elevation as possible, too. This is a fun way to experience a bird's-eye view of where you live in a tangible way. You could also try doing this with another country.

5. Invite a missionary to your home. Encourage them to bring pictures and artifacts from where they serve. Hearing engrossing stories from someone who's lived in another country often inspires interest in that country. We love to hear incredible stories of how God provides in difficult situations. In this way, children can have the opportunity to ask questions and interact with someone who knows both your culture and someone else's intimately.

6. Try letterboxing. This is an activity that is similar to geocaching but that doesn't require anything fancier than a compass. Basically, you follow geographic clues to find a hidden stash. The stash always contains a logbook and stamp, but it sometimes contains other treasures. The stamp is for you to mark in your own logbook that you completed that challenge. The logbook in the cache is to record your name and the date you were there. There are several websites with letterboxing challenges, with a variety of difficulty levels. They are almost always outdoors and usually take one to four hours to complete. A variation on this is Big City Scavenger Hunts. This company has set up hunts in more than 200 cities in six countries. There is a significant fee involved. Go to their website to learn more. *(I do not get any commission for mentioning them. This is for your information only.)*

7. Why do we celebrate Memorial Day? Do your kids ever ask questions like: "What is Labor Day? Why do we have Memorial Day and Veterans Day?" If you live outside the United States, your kids probably ask similar questions about your holidays. This activity is about finding out the origins of your holidays. Did you know that many celebrations have their roots in Roman religious festivals? We have adapted and changed them, but as you read and discuss, don't shy away from digging further into history. Are there other ways that ancient cultures still influence us today?

Nature and Science

In this section, you will find several game-type suggestions, but no experiments or "lessons." There are plenty of experiment kits, books, Pinterest pages, and the like about specific science challenges and activities. You will find some of these on my Pinterest page as well. Please visit my *100 Ways to Motivate Kids* board at my Pinterest page to see some of my favorites. I hope you enjoy some of these unusual ways to see what your child already knows and to challenge them further.

1. Create a "mystery box." Gather recyclable materials such as yogurt containers and lids, empty thread spools, toilet paper and paper towel rolls, twisty ties, and whatever other things you can find. The best materials are in unusual shapes and sizes. Put them out where your children will find them and then add a special item, such as pipe cleaners, Styrofoam, or wood dowels. Pose a challenge. Say, "Can you make something that moves using the (special item) and stuff from this box?" Think up other challenges, like a marble run or a toy, and continue adding to the box. This uses both creativity and engineering and physical science principles.

2. Play "stump Mom." Every kid likes to feel as though they know more than their parents. My son Mouse thinks that he knows all there is to know about rodents because he has read a lot about them. I might say to him: "You know a lot about rodents. Let's see if you can stump me. Ask me a question." He keeps asking me questions until he finds one to which I don't know the answer. He usually can at some point, and then he feels very satisfied. Because this game uses a child's strengths and causes him to feel good about himself, he will love playing it. This game will let you know exactly how much your child knows about a topic and give insight into how to motivate him further through books, videos, or other materials that can expand his interest. I put this game here because many children know a great deal about their favorite animals. However, you can see that this game could be used for history topics as well.

3. Play "teacher." You are the student, and your child is the teacher. Let him teach you what he knows using whatever props he wants, such as puppets, kitchen tools, plants, or boxes. As the student, you get to ask the "teacher" questions, including ones like, "I don't get this. Can you help me?" See how he responds.

4. Take electronics apart. How do things work? Find out! Allow your child to take old machines apart, whether you find some at a thrift store or have some lying around your house. (For safety, cut the cord off or remove the batteries first.) See if they can identify resistors, motors, capacitors, transistors, and more. Would they be able to rebuild it?

5. And the next contestant is . . . When my children were younger, I used a small puppet named Eunice the Unicorn to host a game show. My children were the contestants. The questions were based on things they were learning about, but the best part was that Eunice was sassy and funny. She had personality and infused the game with her antics. First, I would take out the puppet and Eunice would taunt them playfully. This is an opportunity to use your own creativity. Then, I would set up the game show format, most of the time with science-related questions. While I don't generally promote the idea of prizes, every game show has them. It may be best to make sure that all your children get an equal opportunity to "win" and give the runner-ups a consolation prize, much like the real thing. The motivating factors here should be humor and fun. My own children don't remember the chocolate prizes. But they do beg for Eunice.

6. Create a mad scientist science box. This idea isn't original to me, but I don't remember where I discovered it, because it was so long ago. For this, gather supplies for doing common kitchen experiments. These may include baking soda, vinegar, salt, Borax, white glue, food coloring, and corn starch. Put some "recipes" in paper protectors and include them in the box. These recipes are usually for different types of slime. You may put in a notebook for them to record their findings as well. Leave the box in a place where they will notice it and put a note on it or something else so they know it's for them. Set them loose to try the recipes and see what happens.

7. Become a naturalist. Kids of this age usually have decent drawing skills and are strong enough to build structures. This is not a scavenger hunt activity or magnifying glass activity as you might do with little kids. This idea is more about nature challenges. Here are some for your explorer:

- How many trees can you identify? Draw their leaves. How are they used by humans? By animals?
- Which of the plants are edible? How are they used?
- What nature signs tell you which way is north when you can't see the sun?
- How did the water where you live get there?
- Encourage your child to keep a nature notebook of their findings, drawings, and new questions that come

up (including the answers they discover). Try to allow them to discover the answers on their own. Come up with new things to investigate based on the geography of your area.

. . . .

Art and More

. . . .

Most kids don't need to be motivated to do art. But, if you're like me, you can end up with piles of paintings and boxes of old sculptures for which you have no use. Many art kits try to teach kids how to make something useful, such as purses or belts, but these often appeal only to girls. While completed crafts may be nice, girls often don't end up using them. Instead, they give them to someone else. Here are some ideas that can encourage both boys and girls. Included here are some creative ways to serve others through volunteering and entrepreneurship as well.

1. Repaint an old piece of furniture. Don't use regular stain; instead, get some colored paint. Encourage your children to see the chair, table, nightstand, bookshelf, or whatever it may be as a canvas. How can they incorporate the unique elements of the furniture to express their idea? For example: chair legs can be vines, drawers can be eyes that open and close, shelves can be different floors in a building. Let them put the repainted furniture in their rooms.

2. Random art of kindness. Collect some rocks large enough to write on. Paint something beautiful on each rock, along with an encouraging message (you may want to write the message in permanent marker instead of with paint). Leave the rocks in random, but visible, places around your town or neighborhood and watch folks' faces light up.

3. Make and distribute cookies (or filled, plastic, Easter eggs) to your neighbors. We have done this for several years at Christmastime. Our block has about 35 houses, and I make enough cookies so that each house gets at least three. I put them in baggies with a Bible verse and our name and house number. That way neighbors who don't know us can feel safe eating the cookies. It has helped us get to know our neighbors and sends a message of friendliness and care for them.

4. Adopt an elderly friend. Know an elderly neighbor or church member who is widowed and alone? Even if they have children or grandchildren who live nearby, they may not see them more than a couple times a month. This is where you can step in. Invite them to come with you on outings. Visit with them every week. Share a meal with them occasionally.

5. Hot coffee and a muffin, sir? Many people don't have time for breakfast before they go to work. They either end up getting unhealthy donuts from the convenience store or eating nothing. Your child can offer nutritious homemade muffins and coffee for $2, still make a profit, and offer something that people appreciate. She could go door to door with a carafe and a basket or, she could set up a table in your front yard.

6. Pull your weeds; water your garden. Encourage your child to explore ways to have a little business. It doesn't have to be a lemonade stand. Why not offer to pull weeds, water flowers, wash cars, or walk dogs? Many neighbors would be happy to pay someone they know to do menial tasks like these. Maybe your child could offer to do the first job for free to build a neighbor's confidence in his ability to do a good job.

7. Repurposed art. Make beads from old newspapers or fabric scraps. Make new quilts from old fabric squares. These can then be donated to trauma victims, pediatric patients, single, new moms, or other worthy recipients. They could even be sold as doll quilts at craft fairs. You can also transform old plastic bags into waterproof sleeping mats for the homeless. Check out websites for how to make "plarn," yarn from plastic bags that is then used to crochet the mats. Look for opportunities to use other materials in a new way to help others.

Ideas for Teenagers

Teenagers are very competent and smart, but very often we don't treat them that way. They are trying to find their own identity at this stage. They want to know that what they are learning is relevant, and they want to make a difference. However, many teens seem to be unmotivated to do anything. Help them see that their opinions matter, that their actions matter, and that they are an integral part of their community and the larger world. The ideas in this section encourage community involvement, creativity, and critical thinking about real issues. You may want to show your teen these ideas and see if they are inspired. Show your support and follow through.

Communication Arts

1. What do you think? Ask your teen's opinion about an article you read. They will have to read it in order to offer an opinion and will appreciate that you value their opinion, even if it differs from yours. This can be the launchpad for serious discussion and analysis. Why do they hold their opinion? How did they come to their conclusions? How do generational views affect differing perspectives?

2. See, Mom, I'm on TV! Invite your teen to start his own YouTube channel. To build an audience, he will have to post regularly. To get people to follow him, he also will need to learn how to engage people with something about which he is passionate. My son Hawk lives with dyslexia, so writing is difficult for him. However, he posts videos to his YouTube channel that feature him creating interesting objects from scrap metal. He has learned scripting, audio editing, time-lapsing, lighting, and so much more as he regularly posts new videos. In the comments of his videos, he also gets feedback that helps him improve. Everything he learns is a transferable skill that he could use in the workplace.

3. Write a letter to the editor of a local newspaper about a recent event. When sharing her perspective on a hot topic, your teen will need to learn how to craft a compelling argument with succinct points. She will also need to learn about source materials.

4. What is fake news? Choose a news article or broadcast and try to hunt down the sources for the claims. Are they primary sources or secondary sources? I have noticed that, many times, one magazine quotes another magazine as their source, as in *Huffington Post* quoting from *TIME*. Challenge your teens to find the primary source in government databases and in medical, business, and academic databases and libraries. These databases are part of the "Deep Web," something that many teens have heard mythical rumors about. The Deep Web is something they should feel comfortable with as 95% of the information stored on the Internet is part of it. If they attend college, they will spend a lot of time in the Deep Web doing research for their college papers. The other 5% is what I like to call the "Google Web" as it is the list of websites that most people see when they do a search. Try Google Scholar and you will reach the Deep Web.

5. What does "ROTFC" mean? Maybe they *do* know what it means—"Rolling On The Floor Crying"—but it could just as easily mean something else. Ask them to think about other possible words that could be substituted and could still make sense. How about "Rocking Out The Fun Club" or "Rolling Out The Funky Carpet"? Texting is full of these little acronyms, and even though they are common, not everyone is familiar with all of them. Ask them to think about the implications of being misunderstood in this way. Why not discuss the ways in which these acronyms become commonplace and what that might mean for the future of communication?

6. What is the difference between a blog post and a personal essay? Is knowing how to write a five-paragraph essay even relevant anymore? I'm sure your teen has an opinion about this and you do, too. This is a great topic for debate! Do you know the difference between the two? Look at some of your favorite blog posts with your teen and see if you can decide together how blogging and essay writing are similar and different.

7. Convince me. Your teen is probably familiar with e-mail marketing if she has bought anything at all online. Anytime you make an online purchase, you must provide an e-mail address. Suddenly, you start getting e-mails about the latest sales, special deals, coupons, and exclusive offers at your favorite store. Ask your teen if she has seen e-mails that promote a product, a website, or that tease her with a "read more" button in the middle of a blog post. Can she create a marketing e-mail that would convince you to buy something?

8. What's their story? Some teens like hanging out in cafés. There is something aesthetic about sitting in a coffee shop, sipping lattes with girlfriends. Everyone there is absorbed in their own lives, but each person comes with their own history, their own story to tell. Why not ask, "I wonder what that guy over there is thinking (or working on, or talking about)?" Don't actually ask them or even spy on them. Instead, start jotting down "what ifs." What if that guy over there, who is sipping his coffee slowly and tracking customers with his eyes, is actually a private detective watching for a specific customer to come in? What if those two women leaning close to each other, speaking in low tones, are planning a secret getaway away from their families? Encourage your teen to imagine different scenarios and to choose one to develop into a piece of flash fiction—a story fewer than 1,200 words.

....

Applied Math

....

1. How much money will I need to move out? What will I need on a monthly basis? Every young person knows they will move out soon. Do they have an accurate understanding of what rent costs in your area? How about heat, water, electricity, phone, insurance, transportation, food, and all the rest? What will it cost to furnish that apartment (and don't forget the bedsheets, bath towels, dishes, and small appliances)? Challenge your teen to find out what these costs are and to calculate how much she will need to move out and what salary she will need every month. This is often an eye-opening exercise that helps them understand the importance of further training in order to procure higher earnings.

2. How much does it really cost to own a car? Is it, in fact, cheaper to use car share programs or public transportation? Much like number one above, ask your teen to investigate all the costs associated with owning a car. Make sure he includes insurance, maintenance, gas, the initial loan, and vehicle stickers. There may also be the additional costs of parking and driver's education to consider. Compare the cumulative costs of car ownership with the cost of using car share programs and/ or public transportation. Is it worth it to own a car and, if so, under what circumstances? We live near Chicago and went through this exercise for our vehicles. We ended up selling one of them, and, whenever we need a second car, we usually use the bus, train, or an independent taxi service like Uber or Lyft.

3. I want to own my own business, Mom. That's great, but do you know all that is involved? Lots of teens have great ideas, but most of them don't know anything about running a business. If they hope to run a crowdfunding campaign to get their businesses off the ground, folks want to see a solid business plan. Have your teen find out what a business plan entails and then create a detailed report including startup costs, marketing plan, and product development.

4. How many hours of work does that dress cost? When teens start working for the first time, they are excited to have money in their hands. Sometimes, they start spending it on all sorts of stuff—clothes, shoes, books, music, electronics, games, and other consumables. After a while, it seems like money goes through their hands like water, and then they complain they are broke. Where did all that money go? Well, have them do this exercise. Ask, "How many hours did you have to work to be able to buy that (fill in the blank)?" They often don't think about the fact that they had to work five to seven hours to be able to buy that one new dress, that new game, or that evening out with friends. Was that item worth working all those hours for? Like activities 1 and 2 above, teens gain perspective by doing the math. Have them do this for even little things, like getting coffee at a coffee shop. Is that fancy coffee drink worth working for a half hour? Remind them that for someone who makes $40 per hour, a coffee drink represents only 7.5 *minutes* of work.

5. In twenty years, I'll be a millionaire! Every kid wants to know about wealth. Everyone either admires or scorns those who have a lot of money. However, very few actually know how those folks built their wealth. How did Warren Buffet become such a rich man? Read his books. Want to know how a person who has almost nothing can become rich? Read Robert Kiyosaki's book *Rich Dad Poor Dad*. Talk with your teen about the principles she learns from these books. How do they mesh with Biblical stewardship? There are many Biblical figures who were wealthy. What could modern wealthy Christians do to further the kingdom of God if all of them tithed?

6. Mock stock market. Anyone can start investing with as little as $5 a month. Your teen can pretend to invest in the stock market and calculate if he is losing or growing his money. Ask him to research some growing businesses. Have him choose three to five stocks and start with $100 in each one. He can create a table or spreadsheet to track their performance over a few months. How did he do? Based on this exercise, how might these stocks perform over a year? Investigate how these stocks did last year and over the previous five years. Discuss what factors might influence the rise and fall of stock.

7. What can I do with $37,500? Believe it or not, that is the average debt burden of a college graduate. The opportunity cost of not working for four years is $60,000 to $115,000 depending on where you live and what type of work you might do with only a high school diploma. My point is not to discourage your teen from attending college, but to think carefully about this choice. Is the degree worth the opportunity cost and the debt? What could he do with $37,500 if he chose not to go? If he invested it, how much money would he have after four years? What if he used it to travel the world or to spend a year on a mission trip? What about conferences and intensives to learn marketable new skills?

Have these ideas inspired you? Share your thoughts! Write a review on your favorite bookstore's website.

History and Culture

1. Conduct street interviews. When media pundits say there is a problem with police brutality and racism, interview some African Americans and interview some police officers. What are their experiences? Another topic for street interviews could be: Why are people homeless? Talk with those who are homeless and with those who serve the homeless, like PADS (Public Action to Deliver Shelter). When media is trying to sway public opinion about something, talk to the people who are involved and who are affected. Does everyone think that way?

2. Organize an immersive cultural experience. Compassion International often hosts cultural immersion experiences for families so they can see what everyday life is like for some of the children in their sponsorship program. Your teen could lead one of these in partnership with their friends and with Compassion. This is not a "play" activity, as you might do with 6 to 7 year-olds; it will require a group in order to do it well. Compassion International's 90-minute Give Back Day activities are particularly relevant to helping your church understand world poverty and the difficult choices families must make every day. Compassion makes this easy, as their materials are free, but your teen and her friends could do something on their own as well.

3. Ask to apprentice for a week. Since this is the time in a person's life when she decides on a career, it can be very helpful to learn what people *actually* do. Spending time with a professional who does what your teen is considering doing will help her make wise decisions regarding her profession. It can help prevent wasting money and time. Encourage her to spend time with someone in an interesting profession—veterinarian, computer repair, print shop, etcetera.

4. What if . . .? What if Germany had won World War II? How would the world be different? Take any historical event—perhaps the Battles of Salamis and Marathon, the Battle of Hastings, or the Vietnam War—and consider how the world would be different today if the outcome of that event changed. What language would we speak? What would our government look like? Religion? Culture? Freedoms? Ask your teen to support their imagining with examples.

5. A real friend. In an age of social media, many teens have hundreds of Facebook or Snapchat "friends," but what does it mean to be a real friend? What does a real friend do? What are they like? How are they different from acquaintances? Does your teen have any *real* friends? Some teens mistakenly believe that a friend is someone you hang out with who likes the same things you do. Discuss how he might develop some true friendships and what that would look like. Don't let your teen become one of the many who suffer from loneliness even though they are surrounded by people and have 1,000 Facebook friends.

6. "Those who cannot remember the past are condemned to repeat it." That quote is attributed to George Santayana, a writer and philosopher from the early 20th century. You have probably heard it before and may even have quoted it to justify the study of history. *But is it true?* Can your teen give examples to support or refute this claim? What happens to a culture when their books and artifacts are burned?

7. The Cycle of Nations. Sir Alexander Fraser Tytler, a Scottish jurist and historian, observed that all nations and empires go through this cycle. Ask your teen to discover what this cycle is and apply it to great empires throughout history, including pagan ones. What about the British Empire? What about the United States? Russia? Where are these nations in that cycle right now? What general predictions for the future can your teen make about these nations?

8. "Without geography, you're nowhere." This quote is commonly attributed to Jimmy Buffett, an American music artist. Geography has played a central role in many key historical events and even in the success of particular nations. Ask your teen to take a fresh look at history through the lenses of rivers, mountains, and bays. For example, what role did rivers play in American history, both in trade and in war? Why is Japan, one of the most successful countries in the world, on an island? Encourage your teen to see the important role that geography plays in the success or struggle of nations.

Nature and Science

Some of the ideas in this section involve research, and some involve building or experimenting. Obviously, it is easy to use the Internet to do this. While your teen may already have some knowledge of some of these things, I encourage you to dig deeper and to attempt to apply the knowledge to a new problem.

1. Create a museum of science artifacts. Does your teen like birds, insects, or sea life? Create a collection for display, but include scientific names, where the items were found, information about their life cycles and habits, and other pertinent data, just like trained scientists do. Find out what research is currently being done on those creatures. This can also be done with plants. Consider why creating collections is important to science.

2. Solar energy. Make a list of all the ways we use solar energy. How do solar cells collect energy from the sun and convert it to electricity? How does this compare to how plants collect energy from the sun? Challenge your teen to use solar energy to power a small machine. If she chooses to do this, you can find instructions on Instructables for a wide variety of DIY projects, or you can check out www.diy.org to participate in a club environment designed for kids ages 8 to 18 to build and share projects.

3. Could we live on Mars? In *The Privileged Planet* by Guillermo Gonzalez and Jay Richards, they argue that more than 20 different circumstances are needed for life to exist on a planet. See how many of these your teen can come up with on her own, and then research what the others are, or watch the video. In light of these findings, what would we need in order to build a colony on Mars? Is it even possible? Why do you think NASA continues to spend money on Mars expeditions?

4. Maybe we *do* have enough food to feed the planet. Did you know that the average family of four throws away more than $1,000 worth of food each year? The United States wastes 30% to 40% of its food supply in general, almost all of it perfectly edible. In addition, state-of-the-art, indoor food systems are used all over the world. How does Iceland grow delicious, fresh food for its citizens? How are cities using old warehouses to grow food? Why are urban areas key to a thriving honeybee population? What is a tower garden, and how might one use it to grow enough food for a family in a small space?

5. Build a Rube Goldberg machine. This is a machine that involves many complex steps in order to accomplish a simple task. Use your recycling bin and odd and ends to build one. If you would like to see a professionally built one for inspiration, look up the Swiss Jolly Ball, which is on exhibit at the Museum of Science and Industry in Chicago. Your teen will draw on his knowledge of physics and use his inventive imagination to create something fun out of garbage!

6. Can you meet all your nutritional needs from a particular diet alone? Which diet is best for this, and why? Many teens decide to become vegan or vegetarian out of concern for animals or for health reasons. Others eat lots of junk food and don't seem to care. This is an opportunity to compare some of the popular health trends. Encourage your teen to experiment with vegetarian, paleo, keto, and other diets and to take notes on how they feel on these different diets. Does he feel tired? Does her face break out? Does he feel more energetic and sleep better? Does her mind seem clearer? After this subjective comparison, ask your teen to use a nutrition tracking tool (there are several apps for this; I use Cronometer) to see which diet best fulfills daily vitamin and mineral needs. Why do we need each one of those nutrients? What do they do in the body?

7. Natural air and water filtration. How can we use plants to filter our air and water? Which ones are best for cities? Which ones are best for indoor air pollution? How can we effectively integrate plant-based water filtration into populated areas?

8. How do we get plastic and medicine from crude oil? Yes, it's true. Our pharmaceuticals and the vast array of plastic products come from crude oil. Research how chemists do this. Is there anything else we derive from oil? What percentage of oil is used for these purposes versus as gasoline for cars? Discuss the implications of this in light of Middle Eastern conflicts, the push for oil extraction from the Arctic National Wildlife Refuge in Alaska, and current trends away from oil-based products.

Art and More

1. Repurpose old clothes. Don't throw out those old stained, torn, or just "too small" clothes. Redesign those clothes into bags, pillows, other clothing items (such as transforming pants into a skirt with a new bottom), stuffed toys, or organizing tools. Use your imagination! This will require your teen to learn to sew by hand or to use a sewing machine, but it captures the spirit of "reuse and recycle." Your teen could even make this into a business or donate her creations to a favorite cause, such as pediatric patients.

2. Plan a week's menu, shop, and cook. This really needs no explanation. You might want to give some guidelines for planning nutritious meals, especially if your family has allergies or follows a special diet. Help your teen to find the best prices and learn good shopping habits.

3. Teach a class. My daughter Tiger has always been skilled in art. When she was a teen, she taught art classes to younger children for a year. Another homeschooled teen I know was fluent in Spanish and offered introductory conversational classes for young students. If your teen has special skills in art, foreign language, or music, or loves doing hands-on science, she can teach interested young kids and give back to the homeschooling community. Offering after-school enrichment also could be a great help to parents in your neighborhood.

4. Café gallery. Take a look at the walls of local, independently-owned coffee shops. Many times, they feature the work of a talented local artist. That could be your teen, if he is particularly skilled in this area. Ask him to create a portfolio and to schedule appointments with the managers of these shops in your area. Perhaps he will be the next featured artist and even sell some of his work.

5. Hey, I'm Checkers the Clown. People are always looking for ideas for their children's birthday parties. Maybe your teen could provide the entertainment. Does she know any simple magic tricks? Play an instrument? Orchestrate games? Can she bake and decorate cakes? She can let parents at your church know about her offerings and advertise in local child-friendly places where parents hang out. This can be a fun way to use her talents and earn a little money, too.

6. Handmade greeting cards. Even though e-mail, evites, and e-cards have been around for a long time, many people appreciate real cards and personal notes. Your teen can delight his grandparents and friends with his creative cards and letters. There are many books and websites that feature interesting designs and formats such as origami, pop-up, and stamping. He can go further and make his own papers, too.

7. Learn how to do it "old school." Assuming your teen has a phone with several apps, ask her to choose one app to learn how to perform a skill manually. For example, instead of using Google maps or a GPS app, challenge her to learn how to use an old-fashioned map. Instead of GrubHub, learn how to order food over the phone. What would she do if she lost her phone or if it didn't work? How can technology actually contribute to the loss of certain important skills?

Bonus! Commit to a monthly donation. Many teens have jobs and they can make a difference. For a $25 monthly commitment, your teen can become a Freedom Partner for International Justice Mission. For a $20 minimum monthly commitment, he can support your local Christian radio station. For $38 a month, she can sponsor a child through Compassion International or World Vision.

Resources

For additional activities, ideas, and directions, please check out my Pinterest page at:

www.pinterest.com/jpolancobooks

Websites mentioned in this book:
Disclaimer: I do not receive any compensation for mentioning these sites. They are for your information only.

Instructables: www.instructables.com
Dharma Trading: www.dharmatrading.com
Alibaba Trading: www.alibaba.com/Fabric_pid423
Big City Scavenger Hunt: www.scavengerhunt.com

Compassion International.: www.compassion.com
DIY Club: www.diy.org
World Vision: www.wvi.org
International Justice Mission: www.ijm.org

About the Author

Julie Polanco is the author of *God Schooling: How God Intended Children to Learn*, published in 2018. She is active in the women's ministry and on the worship team at a nondenominational evangelical church in the Chicago area. She and her husband have homeschooled their four children from the beginning. They graduated their first child in 2016 and their second in 2018. Julie is a regular contributor for *The Old Schoolhouse® Magazine* and for their *Homeschooling with Heart* blog, and she is the high school botany instructor for www.SchoolhouseTeachers.com.

Her involvement in the homeschool community has included serving on the board of her local support group, starting her own support group, and teaching science and writing classes in her home and in cooperatives. Currently, she maintains a blog that discusses homeschooling, Christian living, and the writing life at www.juliepolancobooks.com.

In addition to being active in her church and in the homeschool community and continuing to teach her children, Julie is a professional freelance writer and ghostwriter.

Visit her website:
www.juliepolancobooks.com
Follow Julie on Facebook @juliepolancobooks.
Follow Julie on Pinterest @jpolancobooks

If you have been blessed by this book, help others by leaving a review on your favorite bookstore website. Thanks!

Other Books By Julie Polanco

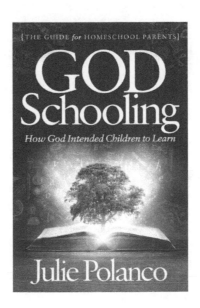

Morgan James
Speakers Group

We connect Morgan James published authors with live and online events and audiences who will benefit from their expertise.

Printed in the USA
CPSIA information can be obtained
at www.ICGtesting.com
JSHW080005150824
68134JS00021B/2289